Salzmann, Mary
  Elizabeth,
  1968-

I am honest.

$19.93

DATE		

I Am Honest

Mary Elizabeth Salzmann

Consulting Editor, Monica Marx, M.A./Read

D1208318

Published by SandCastle™, an imprint of ABDO Publishing Company, 4940 Viking Drive, Edina, Minnesota 55435.

Printed in the United States.

Credits
Edited by: Pam Price
Curriculum Coordinator: Nancy Tuminelly
Cover and Interior Design and Production: Mighty Media
Photo Credits: Corbis Images, Digital Vision, Eyewire Images, PhotoDisc, Rubberball Productions

Library of Congress Cataloging-in-Publication Data

Salzmann, Mary Elizabeth, 1968-
    I am honest / Mary Elizabeth Salzmann.
      p. cm. -- (Building character)
    Includes index.
    Summary: Describes various ways of being honest, including doing your own homework, returning things that you borrow, and paying for things at the store.
    ISBN 1-57765-828-0
    1. Honesty--Juvenile literature. [1. Honesty.] I. Title.

BJ1533.H7 S25 2002
179'.9--dc21
                                                                    2002066408

SandCastle™ books are created by a professional team of educators, reading specialists, and content developers around five essential components that include phonemic awareness, phonics, vocabulary, text comprehension, and fluency. All books are written, reviewed, and leveled for guided reading, early intervention reading, and Accelerated Reader® programs and designed for use in shared, guided, and independent reading and writing activities to support a balanced approach to literacy instruction.

Let Us Know

After reading the book, SandCastle would like you to tell us your stories about reading. What is your favorite page? Was there something hard that you needed help with? Share the ups and downs of learning to read. We want to hear from you! To get posted on the ABDO Publishing Company Web site, send us email at:

sandcastle@abdopub.com

SandCastle Level: Transitional

Your character is the kind of person you are.

You show your character in the things you say and do.

Honesty is part of your character.

I try to be honest.

There are many ways to be honest.

Being honest means telling the truth.

When I tell my mom I broke the glass, I am being honest.

When I tell my teacher what happened on the playground, I am being honest.

Being honest means following the rules.

When I follow the rules of the game, I am being honest.

When I do my homework myself, I am being honest.

Being honest means returning things you borrow.

We will return this book to the library.

My friend lets me play with his horn.

When I am done, I will give it back to him.

I will be honest.

Being honest means paying for things at the store.

I save my money to buy the things I want.

What do you do to be honest?

Index

Glossary

glass   a container that holds liquid so you can drink

homework school assignments that you do at home

horn   an instrument that makes music when you blow into it

library   a place that has books, CDs, magazines, videos, and other materials that people can borrow

money   coins and bills that you use to buy things

rules   instructions that tell you what you should and should not do

About SandCastle™

A professional team of educators, reading specialists, and content developers created the SandCastle™ series to support young readers as they develop reading skills and strategies and increase their general knowledge. The SandCastle™ series has four levels that correspond to early literacy development in young children. The levels are provided to help teachers and parents select the appropriate books for young readers.

Emerging Readers
(no flags)

Beginning Readers
(1 flag)

Transitional Readers
(2 flags)

Fluent Readers
(3 flags)

These levels are meant only as a guide. All levels are subject to change.

ABDO
Publishing Company

To see a complete list of SandCastle™ books and other nonfiction titles from ABDO Publishing Company, visit www.abdopub.com or contact us at:

4940 Viking Drive, Edina, Minnesota 55435 • 1-800-800-1312 • fax: 1-952-831-1632